CW00375468

Design: Jill Coote
Recipe Photography: Peter Barry
Jacket and Illustration Artwork: Jane Winton,
courtesy of Bernard Thornton Artists, London
Editors: Jillian Stewart, Kate Cranshaw and Laura Potts

CLB 3516
Published by Grange Books,
an imprint of Grange Books PLC,
The Grange, Grange Yard, London.
© 1994 CLB Publishing,
Godalming, Surrey, England.
All rights reserved.
Printed and bound in Singapore
Published 1994
ISBN 1-85627-429-2

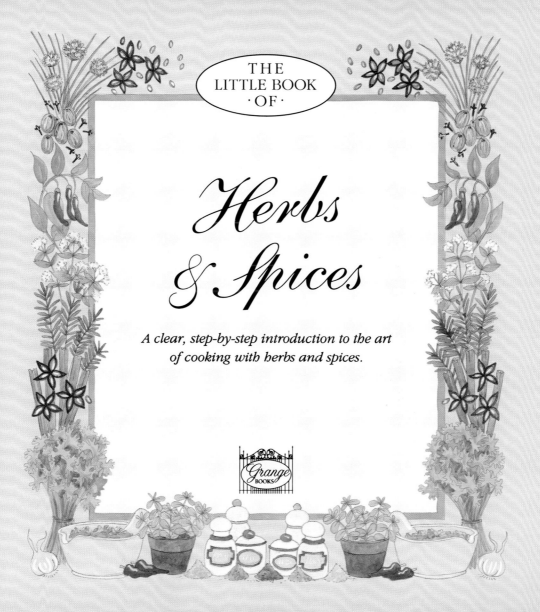

THE LITTLE BOOK ·OF·

Herbs & Spices

A clear, step-by-step introduction to the art of cooking with herbs and spices.

Grange
BOOKS

Introduction

$\mathcal{A}$ few well-chosen herbs or the addition of some spices can transform the simplest ingredients into something special, bringing a depth of flavour to otherwise ordinary dishes. A comprehensive knowledge of the flavours that different herbs and spices impart and how they should be used to bring out the very best in food is one of the greatest culinary skills, and the making of a good cook. Sadly, however, it is one of the fastest disappearing of the culinary arts. Though our forebears cultivated a wide range of both culinary and medicinal herbs and had an extensive knowledge of their properties and uses, the modern cook tends to rely on the dried, shop-bought product, generally growing only a few of the most popular herbs and, in most cases, having only the sketchiest idea of their properties.

Historically, herbs and spices were used to preserve meat and fresh produce through the long winter months and helped to disguise the unpalatable taste of food that was past its best. Modern methods of preservation, particularly refrigeration, have largely seen an end to this use of herbs and spices in the West (in part explaining the gradual decline in knowledge about them) and they are used primarily to give flavour to food.

When fresh herbs are in season and are widely available they should be used in preference to dried, as they are generally – with the important exception of the bay leaf – superior in taste. Basil, in particular, should be eaten fresh as it is one of the few herbs that cannot be dried successfully. Always remember, too, to carefully examine fresh herbs and buy the freshest specimen. As the flavour of fresh herbs can be easily impaired it is important to prepare and use them properly. The oils in the plant, in particular, are easily spoiled and it is these which impart the particular flavour to the food when broken up or heated. To minimize the risk of flavour loss, use your fingers to tear the herbs where directed rather than chopping them with a knife and follow instructions about when to add them to the recipe carefully, ensuring that they are not added too soon or too late. If you are using dried herbs, it is important to remember that they are more concentrated in their flavour than fresh, and should be used in smaller quantities.

Spices, which are the dried seeds, pods, berries, roots, stems or buds of aromatic plants, have played an important part in the culinary traditions of many nations. Like dried herbs, pre-ground spices are widely available in the shops. For the best results, however, it is best to grind your own. If you are buying pre-ground spices do not buy them in large quantities and ensure they are stored in a dark place rather than in direct sunlight as they lose their flavour quickly.

Providing a delicious selection of recipes that use a wide range of herbs and spices, in many different styles of cookery, this book is the perfect introduction to the delights of cooking with herbs and spices. It features some of the lesser-known and more unusual herbs and spices as well as the more popular and frequently used varieties.

Dolmades

SERVES 6-8

These Greek delicacies can be served with natural yogurt or a tomato sauce.

PREPARATION: 30 mins
COOKING: 40 mins

225g/8oz fresh vine leaves or leaves packed in brine
175g/6oz long-grain rice, cooked
8 spring onions, finely chopped
1½ tbsps chopped fresh dill
3 tbsps chopped fresh mint
1 tbsp chopped fresh parsley
60g/2oz pine nuts
60g/2oz currants
Salt and pepper
140ml/¼ pint olive oil
Juice of 1 lemon

1. If using fresh vine leaves, put them into boiling water for about 1 minute. Remove them and drain. If using preserved vine leaves, rinse them and then place in a bowl of hot water for 5 minutes to soak. Strain and pat dry.

Step 3 Spread the leaves out on a flat surface. Place spoonfuls of stuffing on the leaves and make into a sausage shape.

Step 4 Fold the sides over the filling and roll up the leaves.

2. Mix together all the remaining ingredients except the olive oil and lemon juice. Taste the filling and adjust the seasoning if necessary.

3. Spread the vine leaves out on a flat surface, vein side upwards. Cut off the stems and place about 2 tsps of filling on each leaf, pressing it into a sausage shape.

4. Fold the sides of the leaves over to partially cover the stuffing and roll up as for a Swiss roll. Place the rolls seam side down in a large saucepan. Pour over the olive oil and lemon juice.

5. Pour hot water over the rolls until it comes about halfway up their sides. Place a plate on top of the rolls to keep them in place, cover the pan and cook slowly for about 40 minutes.

6. Remove the Dolmades to a serving plate and accompany with lemon wedges, black olives and plain yogurt if wished.

Mussels in Red Wine

SERVES 4

Red wine makes an unusual, but very pleasant, combination with seafood. This recipe is equally good with clams or cockles.

PREPARATION: 30 mins, plus 2 hrs chilling
COOKING: 10 mins

280ml/½ pint dry red wine
1.4kg/3lb mussels, well scrubbed
90ml/6 tbsps olive oil
4 cloves garlic, finely chopped
2 bay leaves
2 tbsps fresh thyme, chopped
90ml/6 tbsps red wine vinegar
1 tsp paprika
Grated rind and juice of 1 lemon
Salt and pepper
Pinch cayenne pepper
Chopped parsley

---

1. Place the wine in a large saucepan and bring to the boil. Add the mussels, cover the pan and cook briskly for about 4-5 minutes,

Step 1 Cook the mussels over high heat, stirring frequently, until the shells begin to open.

Step 4 Remove the mussels from their shells with your fingers or by using a small teaspoon.

stirring frequently, until the shells open. Discard any that do not open.

2. Transfer the mussels to a bowl and pour the cooking liquid through a fine sieve and reserve it.

3. In a clean saucepan, heat the oil and sauté the garlic over a gentle heat until golden brown. Add the bay leaves, thyme, vinegar, paprika, lemon juice and rind, salt and pepper and cayenne pepper. Pour on the wine, and bring to the boil. Cook to reduce to about 175ml/6 fl oz. Allow to cool completely.

4. Remove the mussels from their shells and add them to the liquid, stirring to coat all the mussels. Cover and refrigerate for at least 2 hours. Allow to stand at room temperature for about 30 minutes before serving. Sprinkle with parsley.

Spaghetti with Basil Sauce (Pesto)

SERVES 4

*Home-made Pesto tastes much better than any brand you can
buy in the supermarket.*

PREPARATION: 5 mins
COOKING: 15 mins

120ml/4 fl oz olive oil
2 cloves garlic, peeled
3 tbsps pine nuts
120g/4oz fresh basil leaves
3 tbsps grated Parmesan cheese
Salt and pepper
275g/10oz spaghetti

1. Heat 1 tablespoon of the oil in a small frying pan over a low heat. Add the garlic and pine nuts, and cook until the nuts are pale golden. Drain.

2. Finely chop the basil leaves, pine nuts and garlic in a food processor or blender.

3. When smooth, add the remaining oil in a thin stream, blending continuously.

4. Turn mixture into a bowl; mix in the grated cheese, and add salt and pepper to taste.

5. Meanwhile, cook the spaghetti in a large pan of boiling salted water for 10 minutes, or until just tender.

6. Drain, and serve with the basil sauce tossed through, and a side dish of grated cheese. Garnish with fresh basil.

Spinach and Cheese Pie

SERVES 6-12

This classic Greek pie is simplicity itself thanks to ready-made filo pastry.

PREPARATION: 25 mins
COOKING: 40 mins

460g/1lb package filo pastry
900g/2lbs fresh spinach
3 tbsps olive oil
2 onions, finely chopped
3 tbsps chopped fresh dill
3 eggs, slightly beaten
Salt and pepper
225g/8oz feta cheese, crumbled
120g/4oz butter

---

1. Unfold the pastry on a flat surface and cut it to fit the size of the baking dish to be used. Keep the pastry covered.

2. Tear the stalks off the spinach and wash the leaves well. Shred the leaves with a sharp knife.

3. Heat the oil in a large frying pan and cook the onions until soft. Add the spinach and stir over a medium heat for about 5 minutes. Turn up the heat to evaporate any moisture.

4. Allow the spinach and onions to cool. Mix in the dill, eggs, salt and pepper, and cheese.

5. Melt the butter and brush the baking dish on the bottom and sides. Butter the top sheet of

Step 5 To assemble the pie, butter the base and sides of the dish and then butter each layer of pastry before stacking them up in the dish.

filo pastry and place it in the dish. Butter another sheet and place that on top of the first. Repeat to make 8 layers of pastry.

6. Spread on the filling and cover the top with 6 or 7 layers of pastry, brushing each layer with melted butter. Butter the top layer well and score the pastry in square or diamond shapes. Do not cut through to the bottom layer.

7. Sprinkle with a little water and bake in an oven preheated to 190°C/375°F/Gas Mark 5, for 40 minutes or until crisp and golden.

8. Leave the pie to stand for about 10 minutes and then cut through the scoring completely to the bottom layer. Lift out the pieces to a serving dish.

Szechuan Fish

SERVES 6

The piquant spiciness of Szechuan pepper is quite different from that of black or white pepper.

PREPARATION: 20 mins
COOKING: 10 mins

460g/1lb white fish fillets, skinned
1 egg
38g/5 tbsps flour
90ml/6 tbsps white wine
Oil for frying
60g/2oz cooked ham, cut in small dice
2.5cm/1-inch fresh ginger, finely diced
½-1 red or green chilli, seeded and finely diced
6 water chestnuts, finely diced
4 spring onions, finely chopped
3 tbsps light soy sauce
1 tsp cider vinegar or rice wine vinegar
½ tsp ground Szechuan pepper
280ml/½ pint light stock
1 tbsp cornflour dissolved with 2 tbsps water
2 tsps sugar

1. Cut the fish into 5cm/2-inch pieces. Beat the egg and add the flour and wine to make a batter.

2. Heat enough oil in a wok to deep-fry the fish. Dredge the fish lightly with seasoned flour and then dip into the batter. Fry a few pieces of fish at a time, until golden brown.

To garnish, slit chillies from the tip towards the stems. Stand in iced water until curled.

3. Remove all but 1 tbsp of oil from the wok and add the ham, ginger, diced chilli, water chestnuts and spring onions. Cook for about 1 minute and add the soy sauce, vinegar, and Szechuan pepper. Stir well and cook for a further minute. Remove the vegetables from the pan and set them aside.

4. Add the stock to the wok and bring to the boil. Add a spoonful of the stock to the cornflour mixture. Add the mixture back to the stock and reboil, stirring constantly until thickened.

5. Stir in the sugar and add the fish and vegetables to the sauce. Heat through for 30 seconds and serve at once.

Pasta and Asparagus Salad

SERVES 4

This elegant green salad is a wonderful way of making the most of asparagus, that most luxurious of vegetables.

PREPARATION: 15 mins
COOKING: 20 mins

120g/4oz tagliatelle
460g/1lb asparagus, trimmed and cut into
   2.5cm/1-inch pieces
2 courgettes, cut into 5cm/2-inch sticks
2 tbsps chopped fresh parsley
2 tbsps chopped fresh marjoram
1 lemon, peeled and segmented
Grated rind and juice of 1 lemon
90ml/6 tbsps olive oil
Pinch sugar
Salt and freshly ground black pepper
Lettuce leaves

---

1. Cook the pasta in plenty of lightly salted boiling water for 10 minutes or as directed on the packet.

2. Drain and refresh in cold water. Drain again and leave to cool completely.

3. Cook the asparagus in lightly salted boiling water for 4 minutes, then add the courgettes and cook for a further 3-4 minutes or until the vegetables are just tender. Drain and refresh in cold water. Drain again and leave to cool.

4. Place the cooked pasta, vegetables, herbs and lemon segments in a large bowl and mix together, taking care not to break up the vegetables.

5. Mix together the lemon rind and juice, oil, sugar and salt and pepper to make the dressing.

6. Arrange the lettuce on serving plates. Just before serving pour the dressing over the vegetables and pasta and toss to coat well.

7. Pile equal quantities of the pasta salad into the centre of the salad leaves and serve immediately.

Trout with Chive Sauce

SERVES 4

Chives added to a cream and wine sauce make a delicious accompaniment to trout.

PREPARATION: 15 mins
COOKING: 15-20 mins

4 rainbow trout, cleaned
60g/2oz butter, melted
2 tbsps white wine
280ml/½ pint double cream
1 small bunch chives, snipped
Salt and pepper

1. Dredge the trout with the seasoned flour and place on a lightly greased baking sheet.

2. Spoon the melted butter over the fish, and bake in an oven preheated to 200°C/400°F/Gas Mark 6, for about 10 minutes.

3. Baste frequently with the butter, and cook until the skin is crisp. Check the fish on the underside close to the bone.

4. If the fish is not cooked through, lower the oven temperature to 160°C/325°F/Gas Mark 3 for a further 5 minutes.

5. Pour the wine into a small saucepan and bring to the boil. Boil to reduce by half.

6. Pour on the cream and bring back to the boil. Allow to boil rapidly until the cream thickens slightly.

7. Stir in the snipped chives, reserving some to sprinkle on top, if wished.

8. When the fish are browned remove to a serving dish and spoon over some of the sauce.

9. Sprinkle with the reserved chives and serve the rest of the sauce separately.

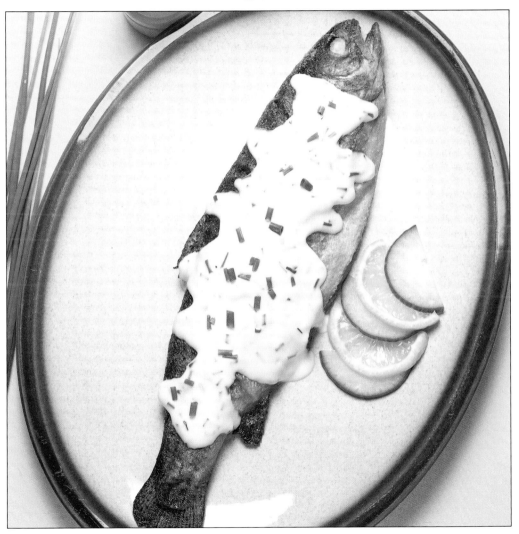

Rogan Josh

SERVES 4-6

This recipe finds its origin in Kashmir, the northern-most state in India.

PREPARATION: 20 mins
COOKING: 1½ hrs

45g/1½oz ghee or unsalted butter
1kg/2.2lbs boneless leg of lamb, cut into 4cm/
   1½-inch cubes
1 tbsp ground cumin
1 tbsp ground coriander
1 tsp ground turmeric
1 tsp chilli powder
2.5cm/1-inch cube of root ginger, peeled and
   grated
2-4 cloves garlic, crushed
225g-275g/8-10oz onions, finely sliced
400g/14oz can tomatoes, chopped
1 tbsp tomato purée
120ml/4 fl oz warm water
1¼ tsps salt or to taste
90ml/3 fl oz double cream
2 tsps garam masala
2 tbsps chopped coriander leaves

---

1. Melt 30g/1oz of the ghee over a medium heat and fry the meat in batches until it changes colour. Remove with a slotted spoon and keep aside.

2. Lower the heat to minimum and add the spices, ginger and garlic; stir and fry for 30 seconds.

3. Add the meat, plus any juice, stir and fry over a medium heat for 3-4 minutes. Add the onions and fry for 5-6 minutes, stirring frequently.

4. Add the tomatoes and tomato purée – stir and cook for 2-3 minutes.

5. Add the water and salt, bring to the boil, cover and simmer for about 1 hour, or until the meat is tender.

6. Stir in the cream and remove from the heat.

7. In a separate pan, melt the remaining ghee over a medium heat. Add the garam masala, stir briskly and add to the meat.

8. Rinse the pan out with a little meat gravy to ensure that any remaining garam masala and ghee mixture is added to the meat. Mix well and stir in the coriander leaves.

Roast Pork in Wild Game Style

SERVES 6-8

The love of game is part of Polish culinary history and even meat from domestic animals was often given the same treatment.

PREPARATION: 20 mins, plus 2 days marinating
COOKING: 2¼ hrs

1.4kg/3lb boneless joint of pork
60g/2oz lard or dripping
Paprika
1 tsp flour
175ml/6 fl oz soured cream or thick yogurt
1 tbsp chopped fresh dill

Marinade
1 carrot, finely chopped
2 celery sticks, finely chopped
1 bay leaf
5 black peppercorns
5 allspice berries
2 sprigs thyme
10 juniper berries, slightly crushed
2 onions, sliced
140ml/¼ pint dry white wine
Juice and grated rind of 1 lemon

Beetroot accompaniment
900g/2lbs cooked beetroot, peeled
60g/2oz butter or margarine
2 tbsps flour
1 onion, finely chopped
1 clove garlic, crushed
140ml/¼ pint chicken stock
Sugar, salt and pepper
White wine vinegar

1. Combine the marinade ingredients in a saucepan and bring to the boil. Allow to cool. Place the pork in a bowl and pour over the marinade. Cover and refrigerate for two days, turning the meat frequently. Remove the meat and wipe it dry with kitchen paper. Reserve the marinade.

2. Heat the lard in a roasting tin. Sprinkle the fat side of the pork with paprika, and brown it on all sides. Cook, uncovered, in an oven preheated to 190°C/375°F/Gas Mark 5, for 2 hours. Pour over the mariande after one hour. Baste frequently with the pan juices.

3. Remove the pork from the tin and keep warm. Skim any fat from the sauce and strain the vegetables and juice into a pan. Mix the flour, soured cream, and dill together and add to the pan. Bring just to the boil, then simmer for 1-2 minutes.

4. Grate the beetroot or cut it into small dice. Melt the butter in a saucepan and add the flour and onion. Stir well and cook over a moderate heat until light brown. Add the garlic and stir in the stock gradually.

5. Bring to the boil, add the beetroot, sugar, salt, pepper and vinegar to taste. Cook for 10 minutes over a moderate heat, stirring occasionally.

6. To serve, slice the pork and pour over the sauce. Serve with the beetroot.

Chicken Moghlai with Coriander Chutney

SERVES 4-6

The creamy spiciness of the chicken is a good contrast to the hotness of the chutney.

PREPARATION: 25 mins
COOKING: 30-40 mins

60ml/4 tbsps oil
1.4kg/3lbs chicken pieces, skinned
1 tsp ground cardamom
½ tsp ground cinnamon
1 bay leaf
4 cloves
2 onions, finely chopped
2.5cm/1-inch piece fresh ginger, grated
4 cloves garlic, crushed
30g/1oz ground almonds
2 tsps cumin seeds
Pinch cayenne pepper
280ml/½ pint single cream
90ml/6 tbsps natural yogurt
2 tbsps roasted cashew nuts
2 tbsps sultanas

Chutney
90g/3oz fresh coriander leaves
1 green chilli, chopped and seeded
1 tbsp lemon juice
Salt and pepper
Pinch sugar
1 tbsp oil
½ tsp ground coriander

---

1. Heat the oil in a large frying pan, add the chicken pieces and fry on each side until golden.

2. Remove the chicken and set aside. Put the cardamom, cinnamon, bay leaf and cloves into the hot oil and meat juices and fry for 30 seconds. Stir in the onions and fry until soft but not brown.

3. Stir the ginger, garlic, almonds, cumin and cayenne pepper, cook gently for 2-3 minutes, then stir in the cream.

4. Return the chicken pieces to the pan, along with any juices. Cover and simmer gently for 30-40 minutes, or until the chicken is cooked and tender.

5. Meanwhile prepare the chutney, put the coriander leaves, chilli, lemon, seasoning and sugar into a blender or food processor and work to a paste.

6. Heat the oil and cook the ground coriander for 1 minute. Add this to the coriander leaves and blend in thoroughly.

7. Just before serving, stir the yogurt, cashews and sultanas into the chicken. Heat through just enough to plump up the sultanas, but do not allow the mixture to boil.

8. Serve at once with the coriander chutney.

Tomato Beef Stir-Fry

SERVES 4

East meets West in a dish that is lightning-fast to cook and tastes like a "barbecue" sauced stir fry.

PREPARATION: 20 mins, plus 4 hours marinating
COOKING: 20-25 mins

460g/1lb sirloin or rump steak
2 cloves garlic, crushed
90ml/6 tbsps wine vinegar
90ml/6 tbsps oil
Pinch sugar, salt and pepper
1 bay leaf
1 tbsp ground cumin
1 small red pepper, sliced
1 small green pepper, sliced
Oil for frying
60g/2oz baby sweetcorn
4 spring onions, shredded

Tomato sauce
60ml/4 tbsps oil
1 medium onion, finely chopped
1-2 green chillies, finely chopped
1-2 cloves garlic, crushed
8 fresh ripe tomatoes, skinned, seeded and
    chopped
3 tbsps tomato purée
6 sprigs fresh coriander

1. Slice the meat thinly across the grain.
Combine in a plastic bag with the next 6

Step 3 Cook the meat quickly over high heat to brown.

ingredients. Tie the bag and toss the ingredients inside to coat. Place in a bowl and leave for about 4 hours.

2. Heat the oil for the sauce and cook the onion, chillies and garlic to soften but not brown. Add the remaining sauce ingredients and cook for about 15 minutes over a gentle heat. Purée in a food processor until smooth.

3. Heat a frying pan and add the meat in three batches, discarding the marinade. Cook to brown and set aside. Add about 2 tbsps of oil and cook the peppers for about 2 minutes.

4. Add the corn and onions and return the meat to the pan. Cook for a further minute and add the sauce. Cook to heat through and serve immediately.

Chicken Escalopes

SERVES 4

Although this is one of the simplest methods of cooking chicken, it is also one of the most delicious.

PREPARATION: 20 mins
COOKING: 12-16 mins

---

4 chicken breasts, boned and skinned
1 egg white
30g/8 tbsps wholemeal breadcrumbs
1 tbsp chopped fresh sage
Salt and freshly ground black pepper
2 tbsps walnut oil
120ml/4 fl oz mayonnaise
140ml/¼ pint natural low fat yogurt
1 tsp grated fresh horseradish
2 tbsps chopped walnuts
Lemon slices and chopped walnuts, to garnish

---

1. Pat the chicken breasts dry with kitchen paper.

2. Whisk the egg whites with a fork until they just begin to froth, but are still liquid.

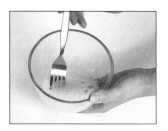

Step 2 Whisk the egg white with a fork until it is frothy, but still liquid.

Step 5 Press the bread-crumb mixture onto the chicken breasts, making sure that they are covered evenly.

3. Carefully brush all surfaces of the chicken breasts with the beaten egg white.

4. Put the breadcrumbs onto a shallow plate and mix in the chopped sage and seasoning.

5. Place the chicken breasts, one at a time, onto the crumbs, and carefully press the mixture onto the chicken.

6. Heat the oil in a large frying pan, and gently sauté the prepared chicken breasts on each side for 6-8 minutes, or until they are lightly golden and tender. Set them aside, and keep warm.

7. Mix all the remaining ingredients except for the garnish, in a small bowl, whisking well to blend the yogurt and mayonnaise evenly.

8. Place the cooked chicken breasts on a serving dish, and spoon a little of the sauce over. Serve garnished with the lemon slices and additional chopped nuts.

Herb Rice Pilaff

SERVES 6

Fresh herbs are a must for this rice dish, but use whatever mixture suits your taste or complements the main course.

PREPARATION: 20 mins
COOKING: 20-25 mins

---

2 tbsps oil
30g/1oz butter
175g/6oz uncooked long-grain rice
570ml/1 pint boiling water
Pinch salt and pepper
90g/3oz mixed chopped fresh herbs (parsley,
    thyme, marjoram, basil)
1 small bunch spring onions, finely chopped

---

1. Heat the oil in a large, heavy-based saucepan and add the butter. When foaming,

Step 1 Cook the rice in the oil and butter until it begins to turn opaque.

Step 3 Cook very gently for about 20 minutes, or until all the liquid has been absorbed by the rice and the grains are tender.

add the rice and cook over a moderate heat for about 2 minutes, stirring constantly.

2. When the rice begins to look opaque, add the water, salt and pepper and bring to the boil, stirring occasionally.

3. Cover the pan and reduce the heat. Simmer very gently, without stirring, for about 20 minutes or until all the liquid has been absorbed and the rice is tender.

4. Chop the herbs very finely and stir into the rice along with the chopped spring onions. Cover the pan and leave to stand for about 5 minutes before serving.

Herbed Vegetable Strips

SERVES 4

Fresh basil and parsley mixed with tender-crisp vegetables and nuts make a delicious side dish.

PREPARATION: 30-40 mins
COOKING: 10 mins

---

2 large courgettes, ends trimmed
2 medium carrots, peeled
1 large or 2 small leeks, trimmed, halved and
    well washed
120g/4oz walnuts
1 small onion, chopped
2 tbsps chopped parsley
2 tbsps chopped basil
280-420ml/½-¾ pint olive oil
Salt and pepper

---

1. Cut the courgettes and carrots into long, thin slices with a mandolin or by hand. A food processor will work but the slices will be short.

2. Cut the leeks into lengths the same size as the courgettes and carrots. Make sure the leeks are well rinsed in between all layers. Cut into long, thin strips.

3. Using a large, sharp knife, cut the courgette and carrot slices into long, thin strips about the thickness of 2 matchsticks. The julienne blade of a food processor will produce strips that are too fine to use.

4. Place the carrot strips in a pan of boiling salted water and cook for about 3-4 minutes or until tender-crisp. Drain and rinse under cold

Step 3 Stack up several lengths of courgette and carrot and cut into long julienne strips.

water. Cook the courgette strips separately for about 2-3 minutes and add the leek strips during the last minute of cooking. Drain and rinse the vegetables and leave with the carrots to drain dry.

5. Place the walnuts, onion, parsley and basil in the bowl of a food processor or in a blender and chop finely.

6. Reserve about 3 tbsps of the olive oil for later use. With the machine running, pour the rest of the oil through the funnel in a thin, steady stream. Use enough oil to bring the mixture to the consistency of mayonnaise. Add seasoning to taste.

7. Heat the reserved oil in a large pan and add the vegetables. Season and toss over moderate heat until heated through. Add the herb and walnut sauce and toss gently to coat the vegetables. Serve immediately.

Spiced Crème Brûlée

SERVES 4
These rich, creamy desserts make a perfect end to a dinner party.

PREPARATION: 15 mins
COOKING: 20 mins

---

4 egg yolks
1½ tbsps cornflour
90g/3oz sugar
280ml/½ pint milk
280ml/½ pint double cream
1 stick cinnamon
2 tsps coriander seed, slightly crushed
1 vanilla pod
Demerara sugar

---

1. Beat the egg yolks, cornflour and sugar together until pale.

2. Heat the milk, cream, spices and vanilla just to boiling point then gradually strain onto the egg yolk mixture, beating constantly.

3. Return the custard to the rinsed-out pan and place over a gentle heat. Bring the mixture to the boil, stirring constantly.

4. When the mixture coats the back of the spoon remove from the heat. Do not allow to boil rapidly.

5. Strain into 4 ramekin dishes. The custard should come almost to the top. Chill until set.

6. Put the custards into a roasting tin and surround with ice. Sprinkle a thin layer of the demerara sugar over the top of each custard and put under a very hot grill.

7. Rotate the dishes and move the tin around until the sugar melts and caramelizes.

8. Chill until the sugar layer is hard and crisp.

Guava Mint Sorbet

MAKES 850ml/1½ pints
The exotic taste of guava works well with mint.

PREPARATION: 2-3 hrs, including freezing

175g/6oz granulated sugar
280ml/½ pint water
4 ripe guavas
2 tbsps chopped fresh mint
Freshly squeezed lime juice
1 egg white
Fresh mint leaves, for decoration

1. Combine the sugar and water in a heavy-based saucepan and bring slowly to the boil to dissolve the sugar. When the mixture is a clear syrup, boil rapidly for 30 seconds. Allow to cool to room temperature and then chill in the refrigerator.

2. Cut the guavas in half and scoop out the

Step 3 Freeze the mixture until slushy and then process to break up the ice crystals.

Step 4 Process the frozen mixture again and gradually work in the egg white.

pulp. Discard the skins and seeds and purée the fruit in a food processor until smooth. Add the mint and combine with the cold syrup. Add lime juice until the right balance of sweetness is reached.

3. Pour the mixture into a shallow container and freeze until slushy. Process again to break up the ice crystals and then freeze until firm.

4. Whisk the egg white until stiff but not dry. Process the sorbet again and when smooth, fold in the egg white. Freeze again until firm.

5. Remove from the freezer 15 minutes before serving and keep in the refrigerator.

6. Scoop out and decorate each serving with mint leaves.

Cinnamon Cœur à la Crème with Raspberry Sauce

SERVES 4

Delicious cinnamon creams are complemented delightfully by the sharp raspberry sauce.

PREPARATION: 15 mins, plus 8 hrs chilling

225g/8oz cream cheese
400ml/12 fl oz whipping cream
120g/4oz icing sugar, sifted
2 tsps ground cinnamon
225g/8oz fresh raspberries

Step 6 Stand the Coeur à la Crème moulds on a rack over a tray to collect the drips when refrigerated.

1. Put the cream cheese into a large bowl along with 60ml/4 tbsps of the cream. Whisk with an electric mixer until the mixture is light and fluffy.

2. Mix in 90g/3oz of the icing sugar and the cinnamon, stirring well until all ingredients are well blended.

3. Whip the remaining cream until it forms soft peaks, then fold into the cheese mixture with a metal spoon.

4. Line four individual Cœur à la Crème moulds with dampened muslin or clean damp J-cloths, extending the material beyond the edges of the moulds.

5. Spoon the cheese mixture into the moulds and spread out evenly, pressing down well to remove any air bubbles.

6. Fold the overlapping edges of the cloth over the top of the mixture, and refrigerate the moulds on a rack placed over a tray, for at least 8 hours.

7. Purée the raspberries in a liquidiser or food processor, and press through a nylon sieve to remove all the seeds. Blend in the remaining icing sugar to sweeten.

8. Turn out the moulds onto four dessert plates, and carefully remove the cloth. Spoon a little of the sauce over each heart and serve the remainder separately.

Chocolate Spice Cake

MAKES 1 × 20CM/8 INCH CAKE

What a difference! The addition of spices sets this cake apart from ordinary chocolate cakes.

PREPARATION: 30 mins
COOKING: 40-45 mins

---

5 eggs, separated
175g/6oz caster sugar
90g/3oz plain chocolate, melted
90g/3oz plain flour
½ tsp ground nutmeg
½ tsp ground cinnamon } sifted together
½ tsp ground cloves

Topping
1 tbsp icing sugar
1 tsp ground cinnamon

---

1. Grease and line a 20cm/8-inch spring-form cake tin with greaseproof paper.

2. Brush the paper with melted butter and dust with a little flour.

Step 3 Whisk the egg yolks and sugar together vigorously, until they are thick and creamy.

Step 8 Mix together the icing sugar and cinnamon and sieve this over the cake.

3. Put the egg yolks and sugar into a mixing bowl and whisk vigourously until the mixture is thick and creamy.

4. Stir in the melted chocolate and fold in the flour and spices using a metal spoon.

5. Whisk the egg whites until they form soft peaks. Fold these carefully into the chocolate mixture.

6. Pour the cake mixture into the prepared tin and bake in a pre-heated oven at 180°C/350°F/ Gas Mark 4, for 40-45 minutes, or until a skewer inserted into the middle of the cake comes out clean.

7. Leave the cake to cool in the tin for 10 minutes, then turn out onto a wire rack and leave to cool completely.

8. Mix together the icing sugar and cinnamon. Sieve this over the top of the cake, before serving.

Index